HOW LOVE GROWS

**BY
J. C. HEDGECOCK**

Published by:
J. C. Hedgecock Publications
P. O. Box 702981
Tulsa, Oklahoma 74170 USA

Scripture noted by chapter and verse are quoted from the AMPLIFIED BIBLE, EXPANDED EDITION (AMP) or THE HOLY BIBLE, KING JAMES VERSION (KJV) as noted.

How Love Grows
Copyright © 2000 by J. C. Hedgecock
P.O. Box 702981 Tulsa, Oklahoma 74170

Published by J. C. Hedgecock Publications.
P.O. Box 702981 Tulsa, Oklahoma 74170

ALL RIGHTS RESERVED.
No part of this book may be reproduced in any form without written permission from the Publisher.

ISBN 0-945255-74-8

CONTENTS

What is Love?	1
Not Enough Love!	5
God's Love Manifested	7
What God Desires from You	8
Do You Need More Love?	15
What is the Problem?	22
The Answer	27
How Did Jesus Walk with the Father?	35
A Personal Testimony	38
Sowing and Reaping Love	42
Some Practical Examples of Sowing	44
A Parting Thought	55

HOW LOVE GROWS

WHAT IS LOVE?

Love is the fundamental theme throughout the Word of God. **Love is the essence of God's character and the foundation of who he is.** The Greek word "agape" is used to identify the love of God, and it is defined as affection, benevolence and a "love-feast" or feast of charity. Love is much more than what God **does**. Love is who God **is**. His love is so immeasurable, it is called a "love-feast".

Have you ever been to a feast? I think of a feast as a meal with so much abundance, there is more food than everyone present could possibly eat! God's love is so immense, there is an abundance (more than enough) for every individual who has ever been born onto the earth. **He is more than enough!**

Everything God does comes from a heart of benevolence and the desire to give love to us. Agape love comes from the heart, and any reservoir of real love within us originated from God.

The need to be loved and to love others is shared by every person on the earth. This yearning for love was placed in mankind by God. It is at the very core of our reason for living and the need for which every person is searching. This longing for love can only be filled by God himself. **Every person in the world needs a love relationship with God Almighty, who IS love.** Many people would testify that wealth, fame and success never really satisfy the longings of their hearts, because what they really long for is to be loved completely. Even when the world would say, "You have made it," people realize that their hearts are still empty and unfulfilled.

Oftentimes, people who are lost don't realize they are searching for God's love. They only know that they feel empty inside and nothing seems to fill up the void. They yearn for something to bring meaning into their lives and they try to find that meaning in addictions, striving for success, relationships and many other things. Yet, the only thing that can fill their hearts is God's love, and that love flows out of a personal, intimate relationship with the Father who created them. **Every person on earth needs a love relationship with the source of love.**

The world doesn't understand God's love. They often don't even recognize it. John 3:16 says, ***"For God so loved the world, that he gave his only begotten Son..."*** that whoever believes on him would not perish but instead would have everlasting life. Only through salvation can you receive God's love into your heart. When you have accepted Jesus as your **personal Savior**, you can experience the benefits of God's mighty love.

The Bible expounds upon the love of God in great detail. This leads to the realization that we can also love him in return. There are many examples in both the Old and New Testament of people who enjoyed a personal love relationship with God. This kind of intimacy with the Father is available to you, but loving God must go beyond mere words. You have to add "works" for your words to have real meaning, because love without the corresponding actions is useless.

For example, you may love your spouse or

children very much, but if you don't <u>tell</u> them and <u>show</u> them that you love them, it doesn't really mean very much. I have been married over thirty years and my wife still likes to hear me say, "I love you" and I like to hear it, too! She is also blessed when I do things to prove my love. Both the words and the actions are necessary.

It is the same way with God. He tells us and shows us that he loves us, and he wants us to tell him we love him and show him our love in return. As the old saying goes, "Talk is cheap." A lot of people say they love God but do their actions agree with their words?

God's love has always produced corresponding actions. God <u>gave</u> us his only Son. Jesus <u>gave</u> his life for you. Jesus <u>healed</u> the sick and <u>raised</u> the dead. When you spend time with Jesus you will begin to learn about his love for you. You will begin to see that God's love is never passive. When God's love is in your heart, things happen! Real love flows when you share with God from the heart, not the mind, and you express that love through <u>action</u>, just as God has shown his love for you by giving you his Son.

NOT ENOUGH LOVE!

God is love, but how do we get his love flowing in our lives? Even Christians, who belong to the Father, often seem to be short of love. Most of us don't have the love of God shed abroad in our hearts. (Romans 5:5) We may have a relationship with God that satisfies us to a measure, but we don't really have enough of God's love operating in our lives. As believers, we desperately need to learn how to have a consistent flow of God's love in our hearts so we can enjoy God's love within us and also have an abundance of love to share with others.

One of the first things you may find out when you try to love God and others is that you aren't able to love the way God does because you are hindered by the sins and weights in your life. (Hebrews 12:1) When you move forward in your obedience to God, sins and weights are quickly revealed, because they will try to hinder you from completing your obedience. If you repent of each of these as God reveals them to you, you can move out and do what God says.

It's important that you realize you can't get in a hurry. As God opens your eyes so that you can see the sin in your life, repent with a right heart and the sin he has revealed will be removed. You won't become "perfect" overnight but you can begin removing hindrances every day so that you continually become more free to serve the Lord.

The more you are emptied of self and sin, the more you can be filled with God's love. When I first began to realize that I was lacking in God's love yet was full of sins and weights, I got a little discouraged. I really wanted to have God's love in my heart. The Lord showed me this little parable that helped me a lot.

If you have a barrel full of dirt, it can't be filled with anything else. If you will take a scoop, spoon or whatever size tool you can manage, you can empty that barrel if you will consistently continue removing the dirt one scoop at a time. Even if you only empty one spoonful each day, you will eventually empty the whole barrel.

That's what I decided to do with the sins and weights in my life. I knew that if I would deal with at least one hindrance or sin each day, I would eventually get the "dirt" out of my life. It worked! I'm not perfect, but God has dealt with enough sin in me and removed enough hindrances in me that I am able to enjoy a steady flow of abundant love and daily fellowship with my Father.

GOD'S LOVE MANIFESTED

1 John 4:8 tells us that God is love. Do you really understand what that means? GOD IS LOVE! God doesn't just love us. He actually is love. There is a big difference between "loving us" and "being love." **God is the SOURCE OF ALL LOVE.**

This love was made known to the world through Jesus Christ, as explained in John 1:14 (KJV). *"And the Word was made flesh, and dwelt among us, (and we beheld his glory, the glory as of the only begotten of the Father,) full of grace and truth."* He was the only example of pure and complete love that has ever been present in human form on the earth. God the Father <u>is love</u> and Jesus is the perfect manifestation of the Father.

Everything God does is motivated out of love. Because Jesus is the manifestation of the Father, the same is true for him. Jesus said, "*...he that hath seen me hath seen the Father.*" (John 14:9 KJV) Jesus came to the earth to reveal to all people the pure love of God. He showed the people that they could taste and see that God is good. (Psalm 34:8) All the good works of Jesus revealed the loving character of God. Jesus didn't wait for people to be perfect to love them. He loved those who were ignored and cast out by everyone else. His love was never passive. He reached out to anyone who wanted his love and the same is true today. The only way to have real love in your life is to have a personal relationship with God the Father and his Son, Jesus.

<u>WHAT GOD DESIRES FROM YOU</u>

The religious leaders of Jesus' time did not understand who he was or what he was doing.

They did not see that they needed his love in their lives. They could not grasp the love that was his very character. In Matthew 22:34-40 (KJV), Jesus explains the heart of God to the religious leaders who clearly did not understand the Father's love.

"But when the Pharisees had heard that he had put the Sadducees to silence, they were gathered together. Then one of them, which was a lawyer, ask him a question, tempting him, and saying, Master, which is the great commandment in the Law? Jesus said unto him, Thou shalt love the Lord thy God with all thy heart, and with all thy soul, and with all thy mind. This is the first and great commandment. And the second is like unto it, Thou shalt love thy neighbour as thyself. On these two commandments hang all the law and the prophets."

Jesus explained the importance of love in these simple statements. **The foundation of obedience to God's commandments is <u>love</u>.** It is the cornerstone on which all of God's other commands are built.

The love Jesus is talking about in these verses isn't like the "love" we often see in the world. Natural affection can fade under pressure and it is often motivated by selfishness instead of benevolence. People often have the attitude of, "I will love you if you will love me, " or "I love you because you are doing what I want." There is no selfishness in God's love and he is commanding us to love him and others the same way he loves us.

God wants your love for him to include <u>all</u> your heart, soul and mind. Just as his heart is filled with love for you, he longs for you to love him in the same way. He also wants you to love others above yourself. That is drastically different from the worldly kind of love that, in the end, always looks out for "number one" (self).

God doesn't say anything in his Word just to be saying it. He has a purpose for his Word, and it will not pass away even though the heavens and the earth will one day pass away. (Matthew 24:35) God is not going to change his Word, and therefore it is imperative that we fully understand and obey his Word.

God's commandments are for all of his children. Even a new believer has been given the provision to enter into the presence of God because of the blood of Jesus Christ. It is in God's presence that you are able to obey him.

God didn't list 900 commandments that you need to obey in Matthew 22. He only listed two! During Jesus' time on earth, there were hundreds of laws in the Mosaic law. Have any of you memorized all those laws so that you don't break one and sin against God? Praise God, we don't have to do that. Jesus gave the two greatest commandments and said that <u>all</u> the law and the prophets hang on these two.

If you will obey these two commands, you will fulfill all that God requires in obedience. Both commandments require that you be able to love: God first and then your neighbor. Of course, God speaks many different commandments to his children but they are all based upon these two foundations. You won't have trouble obeying anything God tells you to do if you are obeying these two commandments about love. However, you will <u>never</u> be able to do what God is telling you to do if you <u>don't obey</u> these two commands, because they are the foundation of every other command of God.

Many Christians think they are obeying these commands. They believe they are loving God and loving others, so they must be fulfilling these instructions. Well, maybe not! Jesus did not just tell us to love. He said that we are to love God and our neighbor in particular ways. It's not enough to "think" we are being obedient in how we are loving God and others, because **we will be judged by what God said and what he meant**, not by our opinions of what he meant.

These two commandments must be obeyed and God gives clear details as to what he desires from you. The Word says specifically in Matthew 22:37 that you are to love God with <u>all</u> your heart, <u>all</u> your soul and <u>all</u> your mind. In order to be obedient to this Scripture, you must love with 100% of your heart, but also 100% of your soul and your mind.

John 14:15 (KJV) says, *"If ye love me, keep*

my commandments." It's not very complicated, is it? If you love God, you will keep his commandments. **Obeying the Lord is the only thing he accepts as proof of your love for him.** The more you obey him, the more you are showing him that you love him. 1 John 5:1-3 (KJV) gives additional instructions about loving God and obeying him.

"Whosoever believeth that Jesus is the Christ is born of God: and every one that loveth him that begat loveth him also that is begotten of him. By this we know that we love the children of God, when we love God, and keep his commandments. For this is the love of God, that we keep his commandments: and his commandments are not grievous."

You are also required to love your neighbor as yourself. You are even commanded to love your enemies! The carnal man is unable to love this way. Only God's love within you can produce such an abundance that you have extra to share with others.

Most of the world is turned off by so called

"Christians" who are really hypocrites and do not have the love of God in their hearts. The problem is that many people have tried to walk in these commandments, but they couldn't. Because they failed, they began to believe the lie that it can't really be obeyed. If God commanded us to do something that couldn't be done, he would be causing us to sin! If he did that, he wouldn't be God! (James 1:13)

There is no excuse for not obeying what God has said. You must accept the responsibility to obey these commandments even if you don't know how to do it yet. If you make excuses for disobedience, you will never meet God's standard. God's standard is very clear. You are commanded to love him with all your heart, soul and mind and love your neighbor as yourself. When you do these two things, there will be no doubt that you are following Jesus and you are a real Christian.

It is obvious from the Word that you are to seek after the love of God. 1 Corinthians 14:1 (AMP) says, *"Eagerly pursue and seek to acquire this love, make it your aim, your great quest."*

It is very important that you have the proper attitude toward love. Many people expect the love of God to "come on them" instead of seeking after this love. John 17:1-3 tells us that we have been given the gift of eternal life, which is the opportunity to KNOW the Father and the Son. It is through this "knowing" that the love relationship is developed, but you must actively pursue it with your whole heart. Those who hunger and thirst will be filled! If you hunger after God and are thirsty for a deeper relationship with him, he will answer the cries of your heart.

DO YOU NEED MORE LOVE?

If you are anything like I was when I began to try to love God, you may be feeling a little frustrated. You probably realize, like I did, that God's standard of love is much higher than you are able to reach. After I read Matthew 22:34-40, it didn't take me long to see that I had a serious deficiency of God's love in my life. I couldn't love God with all my heart, soul and mind and I definitely couldn't love others above myself all the time. When I tried to obey these two commandments consistently, I couldn't do it.

It's kind of like having a vitamin C deficiency. First, you need a good diagnosis of exactly what you are lacking. If you know what you need, then you must get to the source that will fix your deficiency. If you have a vitamin shortage, you need to add extra doses of that vitamin until you are no longer deficient.

If you are deficient of love, you have to go to the source. God is love and you can go to him with your deficiency. Another source of "agape" love is any believer who is walking in the Spirit and full of the love of God. The world will be able to see the reality of God's love when they observe our love for one another. When God fills your need for love, others will see the change in you. God can fill you with enough love that it "splashes out" on everyone around you. Instead of a deficiency of love, you will have an abundance.

At this point, you may suspect that you have a deficiency of God's love, even though you recognize that he is the source of love and he lives in you. You may have tried to love God with all your heart and love your neighbor as yourself but it hasn't seemed to work the way the Bible says it should.

1 Corinthians 13:1-3 (AMP) gives us a detailed description of how God looks at the works you might do and the motive for doing them. When you meditate on these Scriptures, you can see that God's standard is much different than what most people experience.

"If I [can] speak in the tongues of men and [even] of angels, but have not love (that reasoning, intentional, spiritual devotion such as is inspired by God's love for and in us), I am only a noisy gong or a clanging cymbal. And if I have prophetic powers (the gift of interpreting the divine will and purpose), and understand all the secret truths and mysteries and possess all knowledge, and if I have [sufficient] faith so that I can remove mountains, but have not love (God's love in me) **I am nothing** *(a useless nobody). Even if I dole out all that I have [to the poor*

*in providing] food, and if I surrender my body to be burned (or in order that I may glory), but have not love (God's love in me), **I gain nothing."***

This is a very interesting passage. Many Christians don't understand what it really means. All of us would be impressed if we witnessed only one of these manifestations of God's power. **Yet God said these miraculous works, if done without his love in you, are worth nothing!**

Think about it! If you or I could speak to a mountain and it moved, everyone would be amazed. As a minister, I could draw huge crowds if I could interpret all of God's mysteries. I wouldn't have to worry about getting opportunities to preach. Even worldly people would want to hear me if I possessed all knowledge and could answer anyone's questions about any subject. Television reporters would be following me around and I could be the hottest guest on every talk show.

Yet God says two amazing things in these few verses. First, he says you can do all kinds of miraculous works, but **you are nothing** if those works are done without his love in you. In addition, he says you can give away all you have or even allow your body to be burned, but **you gain nothing** if you do not have God's love in you. The King James Bible says, **"...it profiteth me nothing..."**

From our natural point of view, this doesn't make any sense. It would seem that doing "works", especially if they are miraculous, would produce great results. You can do any number of things in the natural realm that produce "good" results, but God looks at things from an eternal viewpoint. He <u>always</u> looks at the motive for why the work is being done.

You can do temporal works that produce temporal rewards, or you can do works from a motive of love and produce an eternal reward. Which pleases God? 1 Corinthians 13 makes it clear. Works, regardless of whether they are large or small, miraculous or commonplace, can produce no eternal results unless they originate from God's love in operation within you.

This is the astounding conclusion from 1

Corinthians 13:1-3. A motive of love and a heart full of love are absolutely essential for you to please God and walk with him. Any work you do in your life, if it's going to have any value in the kingdom of God, must be done in and through love. **If you don't get this foundational teaching properly placed in your life, nothing else matters.**

There are two results when your motive isn't love. **You are nothing and what you do profits you nothing.** The Word of God clearly states that all of our works will be tested by fire. 1 Corinthians 3:13-15 (AMP) says,

"The work of each [one] will become [plainly, openly] known (shown for what it is); for the day [of Christ] will disclose and declare it, because it will be revealed with fire, and the fire will test and critically appraise the character and worth of the work each person has done. If the work which any person has built on this Foundation [any product of his efforts whatever] survives [this test], he will get his re-

ward. But if any person's work is burned up [under the test], he will suffer the loss [of it all, losing his reward], though he himself will be saved, but only as [one who has passed] through the fire."

Verse 13 states that all our works will be tested by fire to reveal their worthiness to receive a reward. If your works are built on the right foundation, which 1 Corinthians 13 confirms as God's love within you, you will receive a reward. However, if your works burn up, you will lose the reward, even though you will be saved.

If this is how God is going to test every work we do in this life, doesn't it make sense that we should be living by his standard now? If he is going to test every work I do, as to whether it originates from love, it seems that I should make the necessary adjustments in my motive <u>now</u> so that my works have eternal value.

I don't want the devil stealing my heavenly rewards, do you? Satan loves to keep you so busy doing "good works" that you never take the time to get before God so that he can deal with your heart, cleanse you of sin, remove the hindrances of your flesh, and fill you with his love. If you really see what these two different passages are saying, you will begin to understand why God is dealing with your heart. He is purifying your motive and trying to get the sin out of your life so that you can enjoy the heavenly rewards he has prepared for you. God wants to bless you with the benefits of his love in this life and the life hereafter, but you have to meet the necessary conditions to receive his blessings and rewards. The condition is simple. **If you want eternal results, every work you do, whether it seems "spiritual" or not, must be motivated by God's love within you.** Every work you do will become openly known when Christ discloses it. (1 Corinthians 3:13). If you begin to meet his standard, you can have confidence that your works will pass the test of fire.

WHAT IS THE PROBLEM?
Let's continue looking at 1 Corinthians 13.

Verses 4-8a (AMP) explain how God's love manifests itself.

"Love endures long and is patient and kind; love never is envious nor boils over with jealousy; is not boastful or vainglorious, does not display itself haughtily. It is not conceited (arrogant and inflated with pride); it is not rude (unmannerly), and does not act unbecomingly. Love (God's love in us) does not insist on its own rights or its own way, for it is not self-seeking; it is not touchy or fretful or resentful; it takes no account of the evil done to it [it pays no attention to a suffered wrong]. It does not rejoice at injustice and unrighteousness, but rejoices when right and truth prevail. Love bears up under anything and everything that comes, is every ready to believe the best of every person, its hopes are fadeless under all circumstances and it endures everything [without weakening]. Love never fails [never fades out or becomes obsolete

or comes to an end]."

These verses can be used to "test yourself". If your heart is full of God's love, you will manifest these attributes. Are you unselfish and kind? Do you overlook it when someone else wrongs you? Have you learned how to avoid being touchy and resentful!? If this description doesn't seem to match the way you are able to show love, maybe you have begun to realize that you need more "agape" love.

As I said before, when I began to study the Bible and found out that God wanted me to love him and others with "agape" love, I simply couldn't do it. I really wanted to love God more and have deeper fellowship with him. Because I desired to love God, I also wanted to have enough love to share with others. I quickly found out that I couldn't obey those two commandments in Matthew 22 because I did not have a sufficient amount of love in my heart. Sadly, I have met many other believers who suffer from the same lack of God's love in their lives. This lack in my own life caused me to seek God very diligently to find out the reason for the lack of love in my life and how to fix it.

For most Christians, there is one main reason why you can't love as you should. **YOU CAN'T GIVE MORE THAN YOU HAVE.** God is commanding you to give something you need for yourself. If you need love yourself, where do you get it? If God is requiring you to love him and others to a measure way beyond what you can do, what do you do?

You need an honest diagnosis of where you are and what the problem really is. You have probably heard it said that Jesus is the answer and we are always the problem. Your Adam nature hinders you from doing what God says. Paul explained in Romans 7 that he couldn't do the very thing he wanted to do, which was obey God. Does that sound familiar? Yet in Romans 8, he shared how he overcame his flesh in order to obey God. God's children are commanded in Colossians 3:5 to mortify (kill) their flesh so that it no longer hinders them. Galatians 5:16 tells you that if you walk in the Spirit you <u>cannot</u> fulfill the lusts of the flesh.

In this case, God is love and you need his love functioning in your everyday life. His love needs to be the motive for everything you do, and you must be able to love God with all your heart and love your neighbor as yourself. **God is telling you to <u>give</u> love when you need love yourself.**

1 John 4:19 says that we love God because he first loved us. Jesus loved you when you were totally in sin. There is no other way to the Father except through the blood of Jesus Christ. His blood washes away your sin so that you can have fellowship with your Father. You can come boldly to the Source of Love through Jesus Christ your Savior.

Only God's children can come into the presence of Love himself and have love dwelling in them. Love is the message that will win the world. **WHAT YOU ARE SPEAKS MUCH LOUDER THAN WHAT YOU SAY.** If you have accepted Jesus into your heart, you have already received his wonderful love, so you have the capacity to give love in return, at least to a certain measure. The fact that you can love at all is because God first loved you. Jesus laid down his life for you, which was the greatest expression of love there could ever be.

However, we all need a **steady supply of love** operating within us and we need that love to multiply until there is an abundance of love flowing in us and through us. John 13:35 says that all men will <u>know</u> that we are his disciples when they see our love for one another. A person who is full of love has no trouble obeying God, and that love will be evident to neighbors (and even enemies) who receive it.

<u>THE ANSWER</u>

God's Word explains what it actually takes for you to love the way God is commanding you to love. **<u>At last, the answer!</u>** 1 John 4:7-11 says,

*"Beloved, let us love one another: for love is of God; and **every one that loveth is <u>born</u> of God, and <u>knoweth</u> God**. He that loveth not knoweth not God; for God is love. In this was manifested the love of God toward us, because that God sent his only begotten Son into the world, that we might live through him. Herein is love, not*

> *that we loved God, but that he loved us, and sent his Son to be the propitiation for our sins. Beloved, if God so loved us, we ought also to love one another."*

The Gospel is very simple, yet there is a wealth of revelation in these simple statements. We are to love one another because **love is of God**. What does "love is of God" really mean? Only the love of God can satisfy and fill to overflowing the heart and needs of a hungry soul. Again, there are only two sources of "agape" love in this world: God, who is the source of all love; and God's children who have access to him, walk in love and have an abundance to share. Love has to be consistent enough to produce a continual harvest of good fruit. The world will not be able to taste and see that God is good and full of love unless they see some good fruit in us.

Jesus doesn't list dozens of things you need to work on to be able to love him and others. The law and the prophets are condensed into two commandments. Obeying those commandments only requires two simple things.

You must be BORN OF GOD and KNOW GOD. If you are a believer, you are already halfway there. That only leaves one reason why you can't love as you should. Verse 8 of 1 John 4 explains it very simply. **HE THAT LOVES NOT KNOWS NOT GOD.** You only know God to the level that you are able to love. If you aren't full of love for God and others, it's because you don't know God well enough. This word, "know", means that you know someone through experience in a personal, deeply intimate way. This level of "knowing" can only come from spending quality time together, sharing from the heart.

As I mentioned above, the only way you can come to know God is to first be born of God. You must have confessed your sins, repented, and accepted Jesus' death on the cross as the payment for any sins you have committed in your life. When you asked Jesus into your heart, your sins were washed away and you received the gift of eternal life. John 10:27 and 28 (KJV) tell us what God provides for us when we are born of him and become one of his sheep.

> *"My sheep hear my voice, and I know them, and they follow me: And I give unto them eternal life; and they shall never perish, neither shall any man pluck them out of my hand."*

Many Christians do not realize that God intends for us to know him in a deeply personal way, but God has given us eternal life **so that we may know him**. He already knows everything about us but he also desires that we know him and the provision for this relationship is explained in John 17:1-3 (KJV).

> *"These words spake Jesus, and lifted up his eyes to heaven, and said, Father, the hour is come; glorify thy Son, that thy Son may also glorify thee: As thou hast given him power over all flesh, that he should give eternal life to as many as thou hast given him. And this is life eternal, that they might know thee the only true God, and Jesus Christ, whom thou has sent."*

The only way to get to know God is to be able to come into his presence with a clean heart so that you can communicate with him and he can communicate with you. You have already been given the ability to get to know the Father and the Son, according to John 17:3, but have you really done it? **Are you born of God but you don't really know him?** The lack of love in your life is the confirmation that you don't really know him in the way he has ordained for you. (See 1 John 4:7 and 8.) You can only have fellowship and communion with God and come into his presence if you are holy, because he is holy. You can only be made holy (righteous) if you will repent of any sin God has revealed to you and **receive the gift of eternal life that he has already given you**. When you do this, you can begin to get to know God.

As you begin to know God and spend quality time with him, you will begin to move into a life of intimate fellowship with him. **There is a big difference between being born of God and really knowing him.** You have to do both in order to love the way God requires. When you humble yourself before God, love can flow between you and "love himself". When Jesus prayed in John 17, he expressed his heart's longing for fellowship with his followers. Jesus paid the price to give us the relationship described in verse 3. He made the way for us to receive the gift of eternal life.

Jesus never meant for your walk with God to be hard. Satan will lie to you and tell you that you can never have a close relationship with God, but God has set the conditions to receive the promise of fellowship with him. He wants to remove everything that would hinder you from having close, intimate communion with him. It isn't a work that is completed in a few days, but you can come into God's presence through repentance and find out what hindrances will move you out of fellowship. As you deal with these hindrances by obeying the voice of the Lord and refusing to submit to your flesh, you will stay in the presence of God more consistently. As you stay there longer and more consistently, you will abide in communion with your Father and his Son, Jesus.

It may seem that walking in love is an unattainable goal. What about the "journey" as you work on maturing in God's love and walking with him? Do you have to wait until you're "perfect" to be able to enjoy the benefits of God's love? Praise the Lord! God sees your heart. When you set your heart to seek God, obey him and develop his love within you, he looks at you as if you have already reached that goal.

You must remember this crucial truth about God. **God sees in fullness.** When God looks at a tiny acorn, he can see all the attributes of a full grown tree. We can only see the outward appearance of the acorn, but God looks at the inside where all the genetic ingredients are that will produce the oak tree.

This principle holds true in the spiritual realm, too. For example, if I get angry and offended at someone, then decide to punch them in the nose the next time I see them, at what point will the Spirit of God convict me of sin? God sees, at the moment of my decision to become angry, the fullness of that decision, which would be actually hitting the person.

When you decide in your heart that you are

going to do something that is wrong, God treats you as if you've already done it. The sin may only be in the "thought" stage, but God convicts you for what is in your heart when you haven't yet committed the act of sin. This is confirmed by Proverbs 23:7. *"For as he thinketh in his heart, so is he..."* God looks at your motive and your thoughts before anyone else can even see that you have done something wrong. He convicts you when the thought first comes because he loves you. He is giving you the chance to repent (turn) before you actually carry out the sin you've decided to do. God deals with you at the root stage so that you can repent before your sinful desire produces a full grown tree of disobedience.

Another example of God seeing in fullness is found in Matthew 5:28 (KJV). *"But I say unto you, That whosoever looketh on a woman to lust after her hath committed adultery with her already in his heart."* God sees your sin when it is only evident in your heart.

On the other hand, this principle also works to your benefit when you repent and decide to love God with all your heart. You may not be able to love that way right now, but God has authorized the way for it to be done. Go to God with your heart open and don't make excuses for your inability to do what he has commanded at this time. Seek the Lord and press toward the mark of obedience. Begin to acknowledge the Lord in all your ways (Proverbs 3:5 and 6) and God will show the reasons why you can't love him and others as you should.

Jesus is the author and finisher of your faith. (Hebrews 12:2) When he looks at your heart, he can see the fullness of your decision to love him with all your heart and soul and to walk in obedience to his commandments. God will start treating you as if you have already hit the mark. He will fill in any lack that you have with his love and grace. When sin abounds, grace will much more abound. (Romans 5:20)

HOW DID JESUS WALK WITH THE FATHER?

You can maintain a walk filled with the love of God if you live in God and he lives in you.

You do this by operating the same way Jesus did. John 5:30 (AMP) explains how Jesus' relationship with the Father worked.

"I am able to do nothing from Myself [independently, of My own accord - but only as I am taught by God and as I get His orders]. Even as I hear, I judge [I decide as I am bidden to decide. As the voice comes to Me, so I give a decision], and My judgment is right (just, righteous), because I do not seek or consult My own will [I have no desire to do what is pleasing to Myself, My own aim, My own purpose] but only the will and pleasure of the Father Who sent Me."

The only way to remain in right standing with God (so that you can get to know him) is to repent of running your own life and let Jesus be the Lord of your life. This will keep the sin out of your life. This causes you to be righteous, because you are obeying the Lord instead of doing what your flesh desires. In other words, you will be operating your life by John 5:30 just as Jesus did. You will be showing God you love him by obeying his commandments, as instructed in John 14:15. This produces a state of holiness that allows you to remain in the presence of God and you will get to know him.

As you continue to obey God, you are loving him with an ever-increasing depth. The more deeply you love him, the more you will know him. As you get to know him more and more, you will also begin to love others to a much deeper level. When Jesus is the functional Lord of your life (which means he is making the decisions instead of you), the love of God will be the cornerstone of your life. 1 John 4:16-21 (KJV) tells us what happens when we dwell in the love of God.

"And we have known and believed the love that God hath to us. God is love; and he that dwelleth in love dwelleth in God, and God in him. Herein is our love made perfect, that we may have boldness in the day of judgment: because as he is, so are we in this world. There is no fear in love; but perfect love casteth out fear: because fear

hath torment. He that feareth is not made perfect in love. We love him, because he first loved us. If a man say, I love God, and hateth his brother, he is a liar: for he that loveth not his brother whom he hath seen, how can he love God whom he hath not seen? And this commandment have we from him, That he who loveth God love his brother also."

The evidence of perfect (mature) love in your heart is that your life is controlled by the love of God, which manifests in obedience, and love for others. I'll remind you one more time! Jesus said, *"If you [really] love Me, you will keep (obey) My commandments."* (John 14:15 AMP) The real evidence of a loving heart is constant obedience to the Lord.

A PERSONAL TESTIMONY

When I first read John 14:15 many years ago, I knew that I wanted to obey God's commandments. I just didn't know how. I wanted a relationship with God and I wanted to love him but it seemed that the standard was so high I couldn't possibly obey it. If you have to know God in order to be able to love as you should, what was I to do in the meantime? I knew I didn't really know the Lord.

This was my problem. God said I should love him, which meant I needed to do what he said. 1 John 4:7 and 8 said that I needed to get to know him so that I could love (obey) him. I could only get to know him if I had fellowship with him and stayed in his presence, but I was full of sin and that sin kept me out of his presence. The sin within me caused me to disobey Matthew 22:38-40. I couldn't love God with all my heart and I couldn't love my neighbors as my own self.

When I began to seek God about how to get to know him, he kept telling me to obey what he said. (John 14:15) At first, I didn't see how that was going to build our relationship but I began seeking for ways to obey God. The first thing he told me to do was to deal with a particular sin in my life. That didn't seem to make sense. How does repenting of a sin count as obedience and how would it allow me to get to know God?

This is what I learned. When you repent of sin that God has convicted you of, you come under the blood of Jesus who washes you clean. Even though you aren't perfect and you still need to deal with other things God hasn't yet revealed, when God looks at your heart, he sees it through the blood of Jesus. Jesus becomes your righteousness and therefore you come into right standing with God. Our holiness is in Christ and when I opened my heart in repentance, Jesus washed me. Than I was able to go before the Father and have some fellowship with him. When I accepted God's ways and his standard without making excuses and began to ask him to reveal my sins, he kept telling me different things to obey. At first, they all had to do with, "Quit doing this thing. Quit doing that thing." Why? Because those sins were separating me from fellowship with the Lord. When I obeyed God by repenting I was able to communicate with him.

I began to hear God's voice more and more. I spent more time in his presence because I chose to obey him rather than follow my own carnal desires, which is sin. Not only did that open the door for a deepening relationship with God, it also shut the door to the sin which gave access to the enemy. Satan wanted to tempt me to sin more so I sure enjoyed getting away from his influence!

This was a process that didn't develop overnight. As I continued to accept the Lordship of Jesus Christ and obeyed his commands, I found that I was able to stay in God's presence long enough that he began to change my heart and my character. I found that the more I obeyed, the more "agape" love increased in my heart.

If you will repent and give your heart to the Lord, God will forgive you by his grace. He sees your heart and the fullness of your decision even though you can't obey everything he commands you to do right now. Jesus is your righteousness. Give God your heart and let him begin developing a love relationship with you. Begin to seek him about any sin that is separating you from his fellowship. Obey the words he is speaking to your heart and begin sowing love to God.

SOWING AND REAPING LOVE

When you consistently obey Jesus, you are sowing love into God. This activates the sowing and reaping principle explained in Galatians 6:7 (KJV). *"Be not deceived; God is not mocked: for whatsoever a man soweth, that shall he also reap."* When you sow love to God by obeying him, you will reap love back from God. **Because God is the very source of love, you will receive love back from him in abundance!** It is impossible to out-give God. God will always give back more love than you have sown into him. As you continue to love God by obeying him, your love will grow and multiply until you have an abundance for your own needs, as well as enough to share with others.

This sowing and reaping principle of love is the key to having a life filled with the presence of God. The more you have communion and fellowship with God by obeying him with a pure heart and right attitude, the more you will grow in love. You will even find that you are able to obey the "hard" commandments because your only desire is to love God with your whole heart. 2 Timothy 1:7 says that we haven't been given the spirit of fear, but of power, love and a sound mind. Mature love casts out all fear! There is no fear in the love of God.

As your love grows through obedience, you will find that you are able to love others to a much greater depth than ever before. You won't be afraid of getting hurt and you won't be offended by others who wrong you. Instead, your heart will be so full of God's love, it will flow out to everyone, even those who have been "enemies".

A heart that is full and overflowing with love is the best testimony to the world that God is real. Love that is shed abroad will touch the hearts of everyone you encounter. God's desire is that you be an example of his love in the earth. There is no higher realm of walking in the Spirit than your life being filled with the love of God. As 1 Corinthians 13 tells us, anything done without love is worth nothing. If you want a life filled with love, start obeying God in everything you do by letting him be in charge of your life. When you sow love through an obedient heart, you will be amazed at the love of God that will begin to flow in and through you.

SOME PRACTICAL EXAMPLES OF SOWING

When I first began to seek a relationship with God, I wasn't thinking about trying to develop my love in order to minister, because I didn't even want to be a minister at that time. All I wanted to do was show God how much I loved him. One day I cried out to God and said, "I want to show you that I love you. How can I show you my love?" He simply said, "If you love me, keep my commandments." (John 14:15) That didn't make any sense to me at the time, but that's what God said to me. I challenged God by saying, "Lord, you give me any commandment you want. I will do it because I want to show you that I love you."

I wanted to respond back to God with what he had already given me. I realized how gracious God is. I couldn't give more than I had and I only had a measure of love, as we all do. Every person can have a different measure of love based upon how much they open their hearts when God pours out his love on them.

For the sake of illustration, I think of a "measurement" so you can get a picture of what I'm talking about. Let's say that at the beginning, I only had a small glass of love. God saw my heart. I was just a baby Christian. If God had given me a ten gallon commandment, I wouldn't have had any idea how to obey it. Because God is gracious, he gave me a commandment I was capable of obeying.

His first commandment was, "Quit doing this wrong thing." I couldn't understand what that had to do with love. It didn't even seem fair or make sense but God was answering my challenge. I decided to simply obey, so I repented of the sin he was convicting me of. Immediately, the Holy Spirit came on me like a wave of love flowing over me.

Before this time, I had been singing and praising God and it was as if the Holy Spirit was being "sprinkled" on me. I remembered that when I broke before God previously, I had felt his love being poured out on me and I wanted to experience that again. When I repented because God said to and I wanted to obey because I loved him, that same flow came over me. It was great!

Then God gave me another commandment. He told me to quit doing another thing I'd been doing wrong. I instantly did what he said and the Spirit flowed over me again. It was the sowing and reaping principle at work! You are going to reap whatever you sow. It was very simple.

If you sow tomatoes, you don't reap beans. If you sow beans, you don't reap corn. I began sowing what little bit of agape love I had and I was reaping love from God in return. You can obey God for other reasons, but it doesn't work because the motive isn't right. If you want to reap love you have to sow love.

I began sowing love (through obedience) into God who is the source of all love. God is very gracious and abundantly generous. You can't out-give God. Every time I obeyed, I got back more love than I gave. When I sowed my little glass of love, I got two glasses back.

When I asked him for another commandment I could obey to show my love, he could then give me a two glass commandment because my love had increased by obeying the last one. This started the process of love growing in my life.

I didn't understand this principle at that time. I only knew I was having fun. I was expressing love to God and he was expressing love back to me. I was able to stay in his presence for longer periods of time. I was getting to know him a little bit and it was fantastic. The relationship between God and me was continuing and his love in me was growing. I was getting more and more excited all the time.

As time passed, I realized that if I obeyed a command that was more difficult, it would express a greater amount of love to him. So, one day I asked him to give me a harder commandment so I can show you that I love you even more. God had one ready! It took all I had to obey that one but his response was even stronger than before. I wanted him to manifest to me in love and he did in a glorious way. I was really praising God! It took more love to obey the harder command, so I was sowing a greater amount of love. Because of that, I was able to reap a greater harvest of love from God. I didn't fully understand it at the time, but I sure did enjoy his response.

As my love grew, I continued to seek God for harder commandments to obey. The next thing God told me was, "Love your wife as Christ loves the church and gave himself for it." That kind of stopped me in my tracks. The love between God and me had been growing dramatically, but at this point I told the Lord, "I don't know how to love my wife the way Christ loves the church." God said, "That's no problem. I do." I started seeking God and he began to give me specific ways to express love to my wife. When I did that, God expressed his love back to me again. As my love grew, I learned to be more unselfish with my wife. I had more agape love for her. She started noticing the difference in my life. As I continued to work on loving God and my life, the love in my heart kept developing.

Then God told me I needed to love my brothers and sisters in the church. We were in a good sized fellowship at that time and most people were really nice, but they were still harder to love than my wife. After all, she loves me and thinks I'm the greatest person on the earth. Some people in the church didn't even like me! I didn't have enough love to start with those people, so I began to work on the ones who were nice first. I started loving them and finally, my love grew to the point that I could begin to love those who "rubbed me the wrong way".

In most churches, there are people who have what I call the "sandpaper ministry". When you see them coming in the door, it seems that the hair stands up on the back of your neck. It's kind of like a long-haired Persian cat. If you start rubbing him from the tail to the head, what will happen to his fur? It will stand up all over the place. Some people seem to have the same effect. It seems they always "get to you" before you can get away from them. If you have a "bear" hiding anywhere, they can seem to find the button that will make it growl.

I used to pray against these people. I would

ask God to convict them for acting that way. It seemed the more I prayed, the more they rubbed me the wrong way. I cried out to God and said, "Why don't you deal with them? Why don't they repent?" He replied very quietly, "Why don't you?" I didn't understand. They were the ones with the problem. It wasn't me! The Lord said to me, "What is repentance, son?" I answered, "Repentance means to turn around." He then said, "Try turning your cat around and see what happens." When you turn the cat in the opposite direction but keep rubbing the same way, what happens? The hair starts to lie down because you are rubbing from the head to the tail. When I turned my cat around, I no longer needed their ministry.

That's what happens when you react with love. It doesn't matter which direction someone is rubbing you. They can rub you in whatever way they want but you just turn your cat around and it smooths everything out. That's what love can do.

As my love continued to develop and I was able to love those who were my brothers and sisters (even those with the sandpaper ministry), I was able to go even farther by learning to love my neighbor as myself. God began to command me to love my neighbors who were goats instead of sheep. It took a lot more love to love goats! By this time, I had more love. As I sowed love into them, I reaped more back. It continued to grow until I reached the level of loving my enemies.

The first time God required me to love an enemy, it felt like my heart had gone through a meat grinder. It was totally devastating. It took me three months to get over that hurt. I didn't get offended at God and I didn't blame the devil. I didn't even blame the other person. I realized that Jesus would have opened his heart to enemies, gotten wounded, and still would have gone out to do the same thing again. However, I couldn't do it! Instead of making excuses, I admitted that there were reasons why it took me so long to get over the hurt. I began to ask God to show me those reasons and I made the necessary adjustments in my heart until I could open my heart to an enemy and I could get over it in three days instead of three months. I kept working on it until I could get over the hurt by the next day. I was then able to open my heart repeatedly and be healed in a very short time.

At that point, God started sending me around the world. Regardless of where God sends me to minister, I begin with my heart open whether they are being nice to me or not. It doesn't matter if everyone in the building is hating me. I can still love them.

When I first started traveling in the ministry, one of the first places I went was a place where they were very offended at American preachers. We were supposed to have fifty or sixty people but about a hundred people showed up who weren't even invited. Their whole purpose was to disrupt the service. They were going to retaliate if I said anything about their organization as other preachers had done in the past. Every one of them stared at me with hatred.

This was one of the first ministry trips my wife and I went on outside of the United States. We were so excited to be there but the hatred aimed at us was overwhelming. I asked the Father what to do and this is what he said. "You open your heart. No matter what they do, don't close your heart to them. You share your love relationship with me. Don't close your spirit or fire back at them."

I have to tell you, it wasn't easy to obey that commandment. When I opened my heart, you couldn't have hurt me any more if you had shot me with a cannon. I had to brace one foot behind the other, the spiritual attack was so heavy. It was hard to even talk. I began to share my testimony for about thirty minutes with hate being poured out toward me. When I got to the part about going through a major breaking before God and crying out to him, and how he poured his love out upon me like a wave, all the people quit "firing" at me. They had puzzled looks on their faces. Within a few minutes, they began to draw the Spirit from me.

As I finished that message, I noticed that it was almost midnight. Everything had gone wrong, but I asked the Father what to do at that point. He said, "Make this statement and make it one time only. ' Is there anybody here tonight who wants to know this Jesus I've been talking about? Raise your hand if you do'." Hands went up all over that building. I was privileged to lead all those people who had come to disrupt that service to the Lord. The Lord also had my wife and me pray for each one and we were there until 2:45 in the morning. People were lined up to the back of the building. They opened their hearts totally and poured out all their frustrations to the Lord.

People had been coming against their church organization for years and had preached against their doctrines. All that did was thicken the walls around their hearts. One hour of someone loving them with an open heart that would not shoot back against their hatred broke down walls that hundreds of years of preaching had only thickened.

That is the power of the love I'm talking about. That is what should be shed abroad in our hearts to all nations. As children of God, our job is to do the same thing Jesus did, which is to destroy the works of the devil. **There is no weapon more powerful for a**

soldier of Jesus Christ than truth delivered in love. Truth doesn't do any good if you can't penetrate the person you're sharing with. It is love that opens their heart. Then you can plant the seed of truth and it will take root and bring forth good fruit.

Allow God to develop this love in your life. Don't get discouraged. If you make a mistake, repent and start over again. Keep in mind--if you sow sparingly, you will reap sparingly. Your sowing is in your obedience to God. That's why you need to acknowledge God in all your ways. Why? It gives you more opportunities to sow love into God. When you do that, you will constantly reap love from God. Your love will increase until your heart is full and you have an abundance to export.

A PARTING THOUGHT

I pray that this teaching has touched your heart. God longs for a loving relationship with you more than you know. He loves you so much and he desires for you to abide in his love 24 hours a day, seven days a week. If you will begin to seek him, you will find him.

(Matthew 7:7, Isaiah 55:6) There is nothing on this earth that can replace the fulfillment that comes from a growing love relationship with your Father.

Additional Books by J. C. Hedgecock

My Sheep Hear My Voice
  Expanded Edition*

My Sheep Hear My Voice
  Children's Edition

My Friends Obey My Voice

The Manifested Sons of God

Light, Light, Light*

Sound Doctrine

The Gilted Prison

*Titles available in other languages.

For more information contact:

In North America

J. C. Hedgecock Publications
P.O. Box 702981
Tulsa, Oklahoma 74170-2981
U.S.A.

In Europe:

Dr. Keith Jenkins
2 William Road
Stapleford
Nottingham
England NG9 8ES